A L L
the
R I G H T
P I E C E S

N A K E I A
H O M E R

**THOUGHT
CATALOG**
Books

THOUGHTCATALOG.COM
NEW YORK · LOS ANGELES

THOUGHT CATALOG Books

Published by Thought Catalog Books, an imprint of the digital magazine Thought Catalog, which is owned and operated by The Thought & Expression Company LLC, an independent media organization based in Brooklyn, New York and Los Angeles, California.

This book was produced by Chris Lavergne and Noelle Beams with art direction and design by KJ Parish. Special thanks to Brianna Wiest for creative editorial direction and Isidoros Karamitopoulos for circulation management.

Visit us at *thoughtcatalog.com* and *shopcatalog.com*.

Made in the United States of America.

ISBN 978-1-949759-49-5

It took a while, but I finally grew into a space that had enough room for the good and the bad parts of me.

Decided I was worth more whole than in pieces.

Saw the value in turning negatives into positives.

Found a reason to get lost in the process of being found.

It took a while but I'm good with me. Grew into a space that was big enough to fit me and my purpose.

Decided that since it didn't break me, I might as well let it make me—or at least mold me into the woman I was always meant to be.

—Whole

We tend to look at the different versions of ourselves and not see the value in the parts we leave behind. We deem pieces of who we were as old, lost, bad... not seeing that those pieces grow together to make us whole.

I've grown to see the value in them all. I gathered the remnants, the stories, the lessons, the wisdom... and I tucked them away.

Now I pull them out for her, for you, for us.

FOR *her*

She took the wood from the bridges that were
burned to keep her from crossing over
and used them to build a house where she stood.
She let the tears that she cried from the hurt of betrayal
fill a bucket she used to wash away the stains.
She let what was meant to break her make her better.
She was nobody's victim.

HER NEXT 4 MOVES:

letting go
healing
forgiving herself
moving forward

She may have gone to bed with tears in her eyes
but she woke up with an "I got this" on her mind.
She just wasn't built to quit.

God is in her.
She's nobody's average anything.

She was confident she could take it
but realized she didn't have to.

She's tired, a little worried, feeling anxious,
overwhelmed, and depleted.
But she still has fight in her.
She's not giving up.

She realized there is nothing she
can do to gain the attention of
a man who doesn't want her
and started saving her energy
for someone who will.

She gets back up
after every fall.

These days she's focused on her purpose, her peace, her growth, her family, her calling, and her relationship with God. That's it.

She stay encouraging others
like she ain't going through her own struggles.

She decided that if peace of mind
living with purpose
growing in love
and staying in faith meant being by
herself for a while
then so be it.
She knew she would come back better.

Don't confuse her need to heal with weakness.
It took strength to face her pain
and say enough is enough.

She made peace with the
pain that grew her up.

She didn't know when or how
but she knew her time was coming.

You will never have to convince a woman who loves herself to care for herself, to protect her heart, to nurture her gifts, to cultivate her purpose, or not to settle.

Self-love sets the tone.

She can keep a smile on her face, her children
healthy, her man happy, her career poppin'...
And still be depressed, anxious, and overwhelmed.
Don't take her strength for granted.

She wanted to say "good," when
people asked how she was doing
and actually mean it.

She finally realized she didn't have
what it takes to be average
and she never settled again.

She's in a long-term, happy, and
committed relationship with her growth.

Her life is amazing because she decided she deserved better.

She finally realized what she
was carrying and decided
to protect it at all costs.

She was unstoppable
Not because she was perfect, had major
connections, or never doubted herself
but because she decided, no matter
what, she would never give up.

She changed her mindset, set some
boundaries, made herself a priority,
started praying more, set some
goals, showed up consistently...
And just like that,
everything changed.

She said, "I'm just not giving up.
The woman I'll be a few years
from now is counting on me."
And the world shifted.

As a healing act, she refused
to agree with those who
deemed her worthless.

She wanted to be whole
so she wrapped herself in self-care,
affirmations, and prayers full of
things she hoped for.

God is in her
She's gonna make it.

She got tired of trying
to save other people
and saved herself.

She's on another level.
You'll have to grow to get to her.

She realized she wasn't asking for too much
and started asking for more.

She stopped saying "this is just how I am"
and stepped into who she knew she could be.

She's bold
She's brave
And she knows how to handle herself.
But she's tender.
So be careful with her.

Her prayers got bigger.
That's how she knew she had grown.

She got a habit of
showing up anyway.

Struggling yesterday.
Strutting today.
That's what the spirit of
"I'm not giving up" does
to a woman.

THINGS SHE'S
KNOWN FOR:

fighting fear
overcoming
making things happen
encouraging others
growth

One prayer after the other
One step after the other
Brick by brick
Penny by penny
Relationship by relationship
Knocking on door after door
Showing up day after day
Holding on minute by minute...
She slowly put her life back together again.

She gave love
She felt love
She was love...
But none of it was
enough until she
learned to love herself.

She had to bend a little
But it didn't break her.

She's a splendid
combination of strength
and softness, grit and
grace, peace and power,
lioness and love.

She learned to tell her story
And there was no more silencing her.

Behind every strong
woman is a story that gave
her no other choice.

Her tests became testimonies
Her lessons became her blessings
Her rejection became direction
Her setbacks became her setups.
She started seeing opposition
as an opportunity to be better
And everything changed.

She loved herself at every stage
Through every season
Past every struggle
On every level
For every reason.
When no one else would, she chose herself.

If you wish to glimpse inside the heart
of a woman and get to know her,
don't bother analyzing what she says or her
silence, her weeping or her willfulness...
You will know her by her smile.
Behind it you will see faint traces of everything
that came to wipe the smile off her face.
If she's still smiling, that's all you need to know.

She's been hurt, betrayed, counted out, forgotten, abused, mishandled, overlooked, undervalued.

She's fallen, failed, made mistakes, made some bad decisions…

She's slowed down, taken a break, fell off, fallen back…

But she's never quit

She's never thrown in the towel

She's never folded.

She's on a mission

She's got a purpose in her

She's got God in her

She's been called to do greater things.

There's no breaking a woman like that.

She's absolutely going to make it.

She decided growing was important
enough to let the excuses go.

She realized that in order to be who she
was born to be, she needed to let go of
who her trauma taught her to be.

She took ownership of her choices, her
words, her actions, and ultimately her life

And everything started working together
for her good.

She learned her life is her responsibility
and that's how she took her power back.

Once she experienced healing in one area
of her life, she craved it in other areas.

The minute she was offended, betrayed, or hurt in any
way, she found herself deciding, in that moment, to
get to work on her own heart.

She gave it to God, she refused to carry it into her life.
She was mindful. She was careful. She was adamant
about remaining whole. Her hurt wasn't her doing but
her healing was her responsibility. She chose healing.

She knew there had to be more to life, and
through faith she believed she'd experience it.

She started dreaming again.

She allowed herself to be hopeful.

She stopped replaying her past and
started planning her future.

She regained her confidence and
returned to her convictions.

She started healing and growing
and nothing was the same.

All of this happened because she decided
to give faith one more chance.

This wasn't easy for her to do.

She had been carrying the hurt around for so long.

But when she reached a point in her life where
it was either her or her hurt, she chose herself.

She worked, she fought, she prayed,
and in the end, she released it all.

And what remained was her.

—She won.

She made mistakes.
She fell off.
She took some losses.
She experienced some bad breaks.
But she had no intentions of going out like that.
She started over again.
Ain't no shame in that.

When a woman has decided to take her
own life into her own hands, and be
all the things she needs to herself, she
lacks nothing. She wants for nothing.

In a moment of growth
she realized it wasn't hers
and let it go.

She's been picking and choosing things that are
not always in her own best interest long enough.

Been making sure others were comfortable
other people were happy
other people had what they needed
other people are able to do their thing.

Now it's her turn.

She's sacrificed long enough

Sat on the sidelines long enough

Cheered others on long enough.

It's her time now.

She needs to be comfortable

She needs to be happy

She needs to get what she needs

She needs to do her own thing.

Some people may be uncomfortable with her
putting herself first, but she's gonna do it anyway.

She's choosing herself this time.

—No apologies.

Protect her heart
guard her peace
invest in her healing
make way for her dreams
cultivate her goals
build her up with words
let her rest when she's tired.

Make sure she stays accountable
increase her prayer life
help her stay in her hustle
keep her skin moisturized
keep her hydrated...

She's been through the worst.

Help her experience the best.

She was done with proving how strong she was.

She was over being at war.

Trauma had her thinking all she was
good for was proving her strength.

But healing taught her otherwise.

She can still take it, she's still strong
but self-love, self-care, and boundaries
taught her she didn't have to be, anymore.

She put all her energy into loving
herself, healing her trauma,
building her character, strengthening her resolve,
growing in God, encouraging other women...
And everything changed.
—Energy

There is more to you than the role you play in someone else's life. You are not just here to be somebody's... somebody's girlfriend, wife, mother... Those roles are amazing. It feels amazing, and is an honor, to contribute to someone's life in that way. But there is more to you than that. Before you were those things, to those people, you were you—you are you. And just being who you are is significant, it's amazing, and honorable.

You ever feel like there's a side of you
that you just can't access?

Like there's this version of you that's way down on the inside...

And you feel her but can't get her to the surface because
there are so many things trying to block her shine?

She's smart and passionate.

Strong and very self-aware.

She's slow to react and masterful in her approach...

She knows who she is and why she's here

She doesn't need validation because
she's confident in her calling...

She is the best part of you, complete and whole all by herself.

And every time you check off a goal you've completed,
let go of something that was slowing up your progress,
and reject fear and doubt, you become more of her.

She has made a home in you.

Keep working

Day by day

Until you feel home in her.

FOR *you*

Stop showing up in pieces

because people can't handle you whole.

If you can't show up with your purpose,
your calling, your skill, your talent, your
ideas, your good wit, your ability to lead,
your light, your brilliance, your past, your
story, your whole self... don't show up at all.

No more leaving pieces of you behind.

3 PEOPLE TO BE
GRATEFUL FOR:

who you were.
who you are, right now.
who you are becoming.

The old you went through hell to get you here.

The current you is putting in work you didn't think you could even handle.

The future you keeps you motivated to heal and grow so you can meet her.

YOU BREAK YOUR OWN HEART WHEN:

You love people who have made it clear,
through their actions and words, that
they don't love you in the same way.

You expect things from people who is
unable or unwilling to give them.

You pretend a relationship is something that it's not.

You settle for what you have instead of
healing so you can get what you deserve.

Let's be clear, you are not responsible for someone
else's actions; and there are things that have happened
to you that were totally outside of your control.
You didn't cause it and you didn't deserve it.

I hope you know that.

But there are times that we unintentionally
participate in our own pain—and uncovering
those times is how we take our power back.

Start believing people when they show you who
they are—and especially when they tell you.

Start seeing yourself in a light that shines on
the best parts of you, so you stop settling.

Identify your core values so you uncover
what you were willing to risk it all for.

Love yourself, so much, so that it
doesn't matter who doesn't...

This next version of you is healed,
whole, happy, and content.

You are wise, experienced, and
emotionally intelligent.

You are confident, loved, and full of faith.

There is no stopping you, no
distracting you, and you would never
entertain the idea of settling.

You are healthy, financially secure, and
operating with intention and purpose.

You are strong but also soft. You
are tender but also assertive.

You have a voice and are not afraid to use it.

You take up space.

You don't play small.

And you know who you are.

Becoming this next version
of you isn't easy.
But it will be worth it.

You should be proud of yourself

For not giving up when

Everything around you

Tried to make you.

You've had some highs, but you've also had some really low lows. You've experienced a ton of losses in your lifetime. And after all you've been through, look at you...still standing.

May you never forget that when
it was hard, and you were overwhelmed,
and felt afraid, and walked alone, and felt invisible,
and didn't have the answers, and couldn't see the way,
and wanted to give up... You kept going.

In an effort to feel love, connection, kinship, and belonging, people will go above and beyond their own well-being just to experience it.

I know they tell you that blood is thicker than water, no relationship is perfect, people make mistakes, and love hurts.

But anyone that causes you to betray your own heart, put your well-being at risk, or love them at the expense of showing love to yourself is not worth working hard for.

No more working hard to repair
relationships you didn't break.

You gotta be willing to lose everything and everyone else in your life before you lose yourself. You can always rebuild, there is room to restore, you have the option to replace, and many things can be repaired. But when you lose yourself, you deprive yourself and risk it all. Let there be no guilt in preserving yourself.

Stop risking it all.

You are not failing, you are feeling.
There's a difference.

May you never wonder if you have a purpose again. The answer is yes. You have a purpose. You have always had a purpose. The problem is that you've been looking for it in your relationships, your bank account, the roles you play, and in the ways other people value you. Your purpose lives in your breath. It shows up when you stand in your truth. It is evidenced by your healing and growth. It resides in your decision to wake up every day and choose yourself. Your purpose is to be you fully, confidently, consistently, in every way.

Stop second-guessing yourself.
You've been through enough
to know better now.

MY HOPES FOR YOU

I hope your boundaries grow stronger
than your loyalty. You've been too
loyal to people who don't deserve it.

I hope it doesn't cost you your
self-love to love someone else.

I hope you see the best in you, even
in the presence of the worst of you.

I hope you learn to believe what
you see over what they say.

I hope your private tears are
replaced with public joy.

I hope you experience a love
that is good in every way.

YOU FREE YOURSELF WHEN YOU
ACCEPT THAT SOME PEOPLE:

will never fully see you
aren't interested in growing
want company in their misery
don't know how to heal

No more pretending you are okay when you're not. Honor your truth, accept and love yourself as you are, and heal and grow into the person you want to be. No more pretending. You need to be okay for real.

YOU KNOW IT'S TIME TO LET GO WHEN:

you don't feel like yourself
you know you deserve better
you're emotionally exhausted
holding on has stolen your peace
red flags are getting harder to ignore
it distracts you from bettering yourself
you've tried to make it work but it still isn't

You're not missing out on anything
that wasn't meant to be.

Trust that there is a plan for your life.

In this season of your life, you are
being prepared, not denied.

Stay committed to your calling. When it's your
turn, it doesn't matter where you are in life.

Comparison will have you thinking you're
failing at life. Don't compare yourself
to others, be inspired by them.

You will get there if you don't give up.

Your past may have impacted and influenced who you are today, but it doesn't have to define or dictate who you will be in the future. Heal so you can decide who you become.

WAYS YOU BETRAY YOUR OWN HEART:

denying yourself access to your softness
by only allowing yourself to be strong

denying yourself access to your joy by
holding on to things that drag you

denying yourself access to your power
by shrinking and dumbing down
to make others comfortable

denying yourself access to your healing by
pretending you are okay when you are hurt

You can love, respect, and have compassion
for someone and still have your boundaries.
Boundaries are for protection, not punishment.
They promote healthy relationships, not
pose a threat to them. Boundaries make
what is allowed and expected clear so the
people in your life know how to love you.

I know how not being where you thought you'd be by now can mess with your head. It can make you feel like you're not good enough, like you've been disqualified, or like you're too late to make it happen. But sometimes you're not being delayed or denied, you're just still being prepared. Sometimes where you're headed is so significant, the time it takes to prepare you for it is especially significant. Trust. The preparation will pay off.

Don't miss your blessing because it
looks different than what you expected.
Release yourself from old expectations
and allow your life to unfold as it should.

You cannot continue to hide
your pain, ignore your issues,
pretend you are okay when you
are not, and expect to experience
the benefits of healing. You can't
heal who you pretend to be.

PEOPLE WHO SHOULD GET
MORE OF YOUR TIME:

people you can talk goals to
people who don't judge you
people who pray for you
people you can be yourself with
people who see you in the future
people whose words and actions align
people who hold you accountable
people who are doing their own work
people who don't switch up on you
people who want to see you healed
people who aren't threatened by your brilliance

You change as you heal and that's a good thing. Don't let anyone make you feel bad about growing. You may have to start over many times before you get it right. Let there be no shame in that. Losing people as you heal and grow is common. Allow yourself to grieve the loss, but don't let it stop your process. If you want something new, release the old. Let yourself experience goodness, even when things around you seem bad. Stop putting off your joy until later. Let yourself enjoy even a small moment of peace, laughter, and love now. Healing and growth may never end. You may always have something to work through. The work you are doing now is building up the strength, endurance, and confidence you will need to experience your healing every time.

Don't allow your age, stage, or status make you settle.
Standards shouldn't have an expiration date on them.
What you've been holding onto is holding you back.
Let it go. Be the kind of person you've always known
you could be. That vision you had of yourself was
to confirm who you are, not confuse you. Grow to
learn the difference between pressure and problems.
Grow to learn the difference between breaking and
breaking through. There comes a time in your life
when you gotta decide to step your entire life up.
Good enough just won't cut it anymore. There is a call
on your life, a purpose for your existence. Act like it.

THINGS YOU CAN
SAY TO YOURSELF
WHEN NO ONE SAYS
THEM TO YOU:

I love you
I see you
I admire you
I support you
I appreciate you
I am here for you
I am proud of you
I am happy for you
I am rooting for you
I want what's best for you

Stop rushing your life because you are trying to
keep up with someone else's. Let your life unfold as
it should, take your time, and run your own race.
You are doing better than you think. You owe it
to yourself. You don't have to prove anything to
anyone else. Keep in mind: life is a series of seasons,
processes, and individual journeys. "Becoming"
never ends, and that's a good thing. It means another
chance to get it right is coming. You've survived too
much to let self-doubt be the thing that crumbles
you. Turn the page. Your story doesn't end here.

Don't rush it, don't force it, and don't push your way through. What is yours will invite you in. You hold too much value to be out here begging to be loved or accepted. Be intentional about building yourself up. Focusing on others takes the focus off you. At some point, you gotta decide to choose yourself, love yourself, and give yourself the best that you got.

Challenge your negative patterns. Deciding that you deserve better and not settling until you get it is the most powerful move you can make right now. Make that move, beloved.

No more working hard to convince people who don't see you to see you. You will never be invisible to the right one.

Understand that what you are doing right now
is for your future. One day you're going to get
a return on your investment. Keep saving that
money. Keep going to the gym. Keep making those
sacrifices and putting in that work. Keep going to
therapy and reading those books. Keep praying
and living fueled by faith. Keep showing up early
and staying late... Just wait and see how it will all
be worth it. Your future is going to be so amazing.

You've mastered making a little go a long way.
You've been sure to make all the little things count.
You've been careful not to do too much, ask for
too much, or expect too much. You've paid your
little dues, and now it's time for you to experience
more. More love, more peace, more joy, more
laughter, more money, more days off, more fun,
more romance, more freedom, more healing, more
growth... More of everything you want and deserve.

It will not be hard for those who
are meant to love you, to love you.

You've been trying to fix yourself
for years and that's the problem.
You can't fix wounds.
You have to heal them.

May you grow to know
the difference between
not now and not ever.

You will find yourself in spaces no one thought you would be in, including you.

When you get there, and you will get there, trust that you belong there.

Don't let your need for closure
keep you from moving on from
something that has already ended.

Please stop wrecking your own peace holding
on to someone who is at peace without you.

Let go so you can heal and
set both of you free.

When it comes to your hurt, you may
not have had a choice in the matter.
But when it comes to your healing, you
get to decide when and how you heal.

YOU BREAK YOUR OWN HEART WHEN:

you love people who have made it clear,
through their actions and words, that
they don't love you in the same way.

you expect things from people who are
unable or unwilling to give them.

you pretend a relationship is something that it's not.

you settle for what you have instead of
healing so you can get what you deserve.

On those days when you feel
unseen and unloved,
I hope you grow to see
and love yourself.

There is a version of you that you will have
to grow into in order to experience.

That's the pressure you're feeling right now.

That's why you are being pushed to heal.

That's why some things are no longer working out.

That's why you aren't sleeping through the night.

That's why you no longer feel comfortable.

That's why you have so many questions.

That's why you don't feel like yourself.

You're growing.

I know how hard it is to move forward without the kind of closure you think you need.

I also know what it's like to stay stuck in a cycle of self-doubt, feelings of inadequacy, and longing for answers that will make it all make sense. When we look for closure, what we're actually seeking is something to make what has become final easier to bear. Or we're hoping that somewhere during the final conversation the other person or opportunity will see our value and choose us. When those things don't happen, we have to grow to choose ourselves and move forward anyway. Closure is a finish, an end, a conclusion, or resolution. When you can do those things for yourself, you take your power back. The problem is in our understanding of closure. It means "to bring to an end." We get closure as soon as it's over.

Stop expecting people to do for you what they have been unable or unwilling to do for themselves. People only have the capacity and desire to do what they can. If they are not meeting your expectations, they either don't want to or really, truly cannot. This applies to things they do for you and for themselves.

You are more than an instance, a situation, a
circumstance, a diagnosis, a memory, a mistake,
a fall from grace, a relationship, an addiction...

You are more than what has happened to you.

You are more than the story of your past.

What has impacted you doesn't have to define you.

You can write a new story.

You can dream another dream.

You can heal from your pain.

You can outgrow your past.

What impacts you doesn't have to define you.

Sometimes our inability to see
ourselves stems from not being seen.

Sometimes the negative words spoken
over our lives are so loud, it becomes
impossible to hear the truth.

Sometimes what we never heard, never
felt, and never saw makes us believe
we didn't deserve the experience...

I pray you heal from all the stuff
that has deemed you unworthy.

A WORD ON SETTLING:

You are probably thinking a lot about your life. You are putting where you are up against where you thought you'd be by now—and the distance, your timeline, comparison, and other circumstances have made you consider settling. Don't do it. Don't settle. As long as you still have breath, you still have time.

Keep going until you get what you want.

Heal for you
Grow for you
Show up for you
Get better for you.
Make it personal this time.

Be discerning of the energy, the time, the investment, the intention... you receive in return for the energy, time, investment, and intention you put in.

Don't go planting your seeds in temporary places and expect to see a harvest.

Allowing people to treat you poorly so you can
prove you are the bigger person is self-betrayal.

Pretending you are okay with something you
are not okay with to protect someone else's
feelings is dishonoring your own heart.

Some people have made commitments to
their small mindset, small behavior, and small
lives. They could care less if you are the bigger
person—in fact, they prefer it that way.

Stop betraying yourself and dishonoring your own
heart to prove you are who they already know you are.

Growth is expansive.

It will cause you to open your mind and heart, widen your range, cover more space, dream bigger, aspire to be greater, and show up in ways that seem massive to those who are foreign to growth. That is not a bad thing.

You worked hard for your growth.

You've earned the right to expand.

You deserve more.

You've lived with less long enough.

Your healing requires your honesty.

Your growth requires your honesty.

Your self-care requires your honesty.

Becoming a better version of yourself requires honesty about who you are, how you feel, and what you want.

Start acknowledging your truth, and watch things begin to change.

Don't be weary, beloved.
You will grow
Through all the dirt
That life has thrown
On you.
—Due season

This version of you may not be perfect.
The truth is, no version will ever be.
It's not about being perfect. It's about being.

May you find strength in the waiting.
May you find purpose in the waiting.
May you find wisdom in the waiting.
May you find yourself in the waiting.

The waiting is not a season of delays and denials.
The waiting is a season of divine preparation.

If you never
get married
have kids
buy the house
earn the degree
conquer the fear
lose the weight
make the money...
You're still worthy.

Your pain is not debatable.

You know what hurt feels like.

Trying to convince people who hurt
you that you are hurt is a waste of
your precious time and energy.

You have to grow into a
space where you don't want
anything that's not yours.

People, purpose, things... if it's not
yours, don't let yourself want it.

What's yours is waiting for you.

Give yourself credit for walking away.

You may look back, you may miss
it, you may even question if you
made the right choice, at times.

But you walked away. That's the
first step towards your healing.

Slowly but surely, you will see the healed
version of you doing things you didn't think
you'd ever do, making decisions you never
thought you'd make, loving and being loved
by people you didn't think you deserved.

Until then, keep going.

Sometimes it takes a while for people to hear you.

But when they finally lend an ear, I hope you have the courage to speak your truth—even the parts that make those listening uncomfortable.

What you expected and accepted before you knew you deserved more was so limited, asking for the basics seems like a stretch.

It's not.

You deserved better then and you deserve better now. To be seen, heard, felt, and understood is the basic foundation of every healthy relationship, partnership, and human experience. That's what you've been asking for in your own way. You're not asking for too much. Get that or get out.

You are not a failure.

When you made unsuccessful attempts at love, career, and other things that mattered to you in the past, you internalized the outcome—seeing yourself as unsuccessful and not the actual attempt. You see yourself as a failure, missing the fact that other people, circumstances, timing, environment, and so many other things also determined the outcome. You are not a failure. What you tried just didn't work out. It wasn't the right person, circumstance, time, or place. Get those things right and try again.

Learn to access your joy before getting rich, earning a degree, being in a relationship, having children, losing weight, having it all together, being fully healed, taking fancy trips, starting a business, or getting a promotion. You'll be more likely to stay in your joy after...

Surround yourself with people who
aren't intimidated when you shine.

Those who are blinded by your
light have sensitive vision.

You're not too much, their
vision is too small.

You need some solid visionaries in life.

People who can stand tall next to your
light because they are always lit.

You need people you can shine with.

People you don't feel tempted
to dim your light around.

Don't dim your light.

Someone else may need it to find their way.

If you knew the truth of who you are it
would be impossible not to love you.

Not the you they say you are, not the you
your circumstances shine a spotlight on,

but the you that survived. The you that persevered,
the you that overcame, the you that is gifted,

the you that is skilled, the you that's visionary, the you
with the good heart, the you with the humble spirit,
the you that is empathic, the you that remains... There
is so much more to you than what you've even seen.
Find out who you are and self-love will be inevitable.

Every time you heal, evolve, shed a layer, change your mind, and grow into a new version of yourself, you redefine your life. You are so much more than your circumstances, what you do, what you look like, or the things you acquire. In life, you are impacted, you are revealed, you are transformed... You are not defined. There's so much more to you.

FOR *us*

THINGS NO ONE TELLS YOU
ABOUT PURPOSE:

you are born with one
it may evolve as you grow
pursuing it can be lonely
it may not make you rich and famous
it will look different than everyone else's
you may not make any money fulfilling it
you don't have to be perfect to access it

Embrace and...

Love who you are right now and work to be better.

Be grateful for what you have and
strive for more if you want it.

Be present in the moment and
have hopes for the future.

Be kind to others and speak your
truth and set boundaries.

Take care of others and take care of yourself.

Give your grace and hold yourself accountable.

Stand in your strength and lean into your softness.

The choice isn't always an easy one, an
obvious one, or one that can be rushed.

But the choice is always yours.
You get to decide when to heal.

HABITS FOR GROWTH:

doing healing work
self-acceptance
personal responsibility
setting goals
keeping promises to yourself
being honest with yourself and
others about how you feel
being selective with who you
choose to surround yourself with

May your boundaries be
stronger than your loyalty.

Release the thoughts, habits, things, situations,
and people that keep you struggling instead
of striving. It's time for you to go higher.

REASONS TO SET HEALTHY BOUNDARIES:

so others don't have to guess what you want and need

to preserve your energy

to establish and maintain expectations
in your relationships

to support your emotional health and well-being

to protect your heart

to prevent you from relapsing back into
old habits and toxic behaviors

so you can heal and grow

Don't discount the work you are doing on the inside of you. While others are getting married, having kids, and earning promotions, you are recovering from trauma, healing your broken heart, and growing in self-love. That inner work counts, too. It's all adding up.

Let love in now
Let joy in now
Let grace in now
Let laughter in now
No more waiting until...
To let yourself feel happiness
Even if it's just in doses.

Allow yourself to outgrow things without feeling
guilt. Growth is progress not a punishment.

Sometimes you don't get what you want because
you have to heal to get it. Focus on your healing

You may have more healing, more growing, and more
learning to do, but who you are right now is still worthy.

Acknowledge how far you've come. It makes
how far you have to go seem possible.

Keep going.

Keep praying.

Keep striving.

Keep pushing.

Love yourself while you are working on yourself.

THINGS YOU GET
TO CHOOSE:

love
yourself
when to heal
when to let go
your boundaries
to grow or remain
to stand in your power
how and what you respond to
what you say "yes" and "no" to
who and what you hold space for

Stop spending your days with
people who make you feel
like loving you is a burden.

THINGS TO KEEP IN MIND WHEN YOU'RE STRUGGLING:

You don't have to pretend you ain't going through it. We've all struggled in life at some point. You have nothing to be ashamed of.

Let the season you're in build up your faith and your strength. When you survive this (and you will survive) you will really see what you're made of.

Protect your heart, your peace, and your energy. Guard yourself from people and things that may try to take advantage of your weakness.

Lean into self-care. Now, more than ever, you need attention, compassion, and tender care.

You won't be in this position forever. Your prayers, daily effort, and resilience will pay off.

Don't you give up. Not now, not ever. One day you will look back on this season of your life and be grateful you pressed on.

Sometimes closure looks like taking
the answer you got, or no answer
at all, picking up the pieces of your
broken heart and choosing yourself.

LESSONS I LEARNED ABOUT
PEOPLE THE HARD WAY:

you can't change a single
soul outside of yourself.

some people will never get you.
learn to be okay with that.

don't get mad at people for
doing what's best for them.
learn to do the same.

you won't find yourself in anyone else.

people will only ever be what/
who they have the capacity to be.

keep other people's opinions
away from your purpose.

people are people. show grace
but protect yourself.

Walk boldly into your healing with conviction, confidence, and power. You've survived too much to be passive about your progress.

ADVOCATING FOR YOURSELF LOOKS LIKE:

setting healthy boundaries
making space for your feelings
honoring your purpose and calling
asking for help when you need it
developing self-love and self-care practices
allowing yourself to express your emotions
going to therapy, seeking mentorship, or coaching

3 PEOPLE TO BE
GRATEFUL FOR:

who left
who stayed
who is on the way

The old you is so proud of
the person you are today.

Learn to access your joy before being rich, earning a degree, being in a relationship, having children, losing weight, having it all together, being fully healed, taking fancy trips, starting a business, getting a promotion...

And you'll be more likely to stay in your joy after...

Sometimes healing looks like crying uncontrollably over someone you lost, yelling at the top of your lungs because of someone who hurt you, or not crying or yelling at all because you just don't have it in you anymore. The breakdown before the breakthrough, the test before the testimony, and the triggers before the transformations are all part of the process too. Stay in your healing.

Sometimes you gotta learn to take "no" for an answer. Standing in front of closed doors for too long will make you think there's something wrong with you— when the truth is, it's just not your door. There is an opportunity assigned to you, a relationship assigned to you, a purpose and calling assigned to you... but you can't access it because you are stuck in the past.

This is your sign to let go. The best in life is ahead of you. Focus on what is working for you and release what isn't... You have what it takes to create the life you've always wanted. You are not being rejected or denied. You are being guided into the right direction. Keep going.

When it comes to other people, it's rarely about you. You get the projections, you get the displaced anger, you get impacted by their trauma responses, but it ain't you. You are just there, available to dump on. Although it's not personal, it's hard not to take that personally. And sometimes it's necessary to give people the distance they need to heal without hurting you. Sometimes you have to love people from a safe distance.

Be careful of what you label "part of the process." Yes, the process may test you, it may get on your nerves, and it may make you tired—but it will not make a fool of you. The process won't cause you to lose yourself, betray yourself, forfeit your purpose, or give away your power. Your process is the series of steps it will take you to achieve your desired end. If there is no achievement and no end to what you are experiencing, it's not part of the process—it's part of the problem.

Everything lasts as long as you let it. Learn to let go. Allow things to pass. Release your hold. Some things need to come to an end so other things can begin. Use your energy wisely. Just because you want something or someone doesn't mean it's what's best for you. Everything that good to you ain't good for you. Some connections need to be broken.

It is okay to grieve what you lost. It is possible to miss what will never be. It is natural to wish things could have been different. And you can still choose to move on. Leave room for your feelings and your future.

It is natural to want to feel loved.
Just don't go shrinking,
pretending, or settling to feel it.

It is possible for someone's best to still not be what's best for you. They aren't necessarily bad for not being able to meet your needs, and you are not bad for needing more. No one should force connections they don't have the capacity to maintain or settle for. You set everyone free when you do what's best for you.

PEOPLE WHO LOVE YOU:

show you with their actions, not just tell you with words

do not cause you intentional harm

make room for your feelings, not judge them

acknowledge and apologize when
they have wronged you

encourage your self-care, not feel threatened by it.

support your growth, not compete with it.

respect you, even when they don't agree with you.

When you struggle to see yourself in the future it's usually because you're looking through the lens of your past. You're seeing snapshots of what you used to do, what you used to think, what you used to want, and how you used to show up. All of that is attached to the old version of you. You're on a whole new level now. You think different, you move different, and you show up different because you are different. Step into this version of you and look again. Your future is so bright.

5 REMINDERS:

you may have made a mistake,
but you are not a mistake.

you may have done some things you've
deemed as bad but there's still good in you.

just because you feel like a hot mess doesn't
mean that you are one. you're doing the
best you can under these circumstances.

you may need some help, at the moment,
but asking for it doesn't make you weak.

there is so much more to your story. turn the page.

When you question its place in your life...

When it takes away more than it adds...

When just the thought of letting go gives you
a feeling of relief...

When it's clear that it no longer wants you...

When it stands in the way of your progress...

When it depletes you of your good energy...

When it steals your peace....

When it steals your joy...

When it makes you forget who you are...

When it blocks your blessings...

Let it go.

Imagine thinking you are failing at life when the whole time you were just feeling your feelings.

Thinking you are weak because you've expressed your emotions.

Thinking you are needy because you are aware of your desires.

Thinking you are ungrateful because you have decided not to settle.

Thinking you are unstable because you are willing to change your mind.

Thinking you are unreasonable because you have standards and set boundaries.

Be careful what you label as failures.

Things take time when you allow yourself to feel.

It's possible to know better and still not do better. You can know you need to change but stay the same out of fear. You can know you need to let go but hang on because what's familiar feels safe. When you don't do what you know you need to, that is an indication that something deeper is keeping you stuck. And until you feel safe, until you feel sure, until you work through your stuff, until you heal... Show yourself grace.

THINGS TO STOP DOING
SO YOU CAN HEAL:

replaying the past
looking for closure
waiting for an apology
pretending you are okay
trying to prove how strong you are
ignore or downplaying your feelings
blaming, shaming, and judging yourself

Hurt people don't always hurt people.

Some of us heal, grow, and live our
lives helping others do the same.

No more working hard to
build long-term relationships
with people who treat you
like you're temporary.

Your boundaries are not meant to threaten, upset, or cause discomfort to others, but that may be the case for those who try to cross them.

Stick to your boundaries.

THE PEOPLE WHO
CAN'T LOVE YOU:

show you what love is not
teach you how to love yourself
make way for those who can

A WORD ON FORGIVENESS

The only person forgiveness lets off the hook is you.
It releases the hold those who hurt you have on you.
Forgiveness is letting go of, or overcoming the negative
emotions attached to an offense—so you don't have to
carry the weight of that energy around with you in life.
Forgiveness makes room in your heart and mind for
new and improved connections. It restores you to your
original place of peace and wholeness. Forgiveness is
accepting that you can't change what has happened and
making a commitment to move forward. Forgiveness
will always be what you do for you, not them.

Strength is earned in the loneliest places, during
the most chaotic circumstances, and under the
weight of a meaningful life becoming a reality.
Strength is a virtue born of much pain. Say
a prayer for those who are wearing it well.

Don't let someone with no vision tell you how to dream.

Some people find it hard to see past their own limits.

They can't see beyond what they've been able to do.

They don't have your heart.

They don't have the stamina to keep
up with where you're going.

Know that it's them and not your dream.

Trust your own imagination, experience, and wisdom.

Believe in your own come up.

Follow your intuition.

Trust the call on your life.

If you have been blessed to see yourself in the
future, it's because you have what it takes to make
it a reality. Stay committed to your vision.

Sometimes things fall apart
not because life is hard,
but because you prayed
for something better.
What you are experiencing right now
could be answered prayer.
Out with the old...

Find a space where you can be you without

apology
shame
guilt
explanation
pretense...

And live there.

You are not lost. You have just been
residing in places you don't belong.

Find a space where you can be yourself,
fully, and you'll feel right at home.

Choosing yourself is usually deemed selfish by those who are used to you choosing them.

This is why you need to do it more often. It sets a precedent for how you want to be in your world.

It makes clear what is acceptable and what's not. It creates a standard for you to measure the quality of your relationships. It opens the door to new opportunities...

Choosing yourself doesn't mean forgetting about everyone else—it means never forgetting about yourself again.

Sometimes we think what we want is too big, that what we want is not for us, but for them.

Sometimes we feel like we're asking for too much, or that we don't deserve what we want the most.

Sometimes we allow ourselves to doubt the existence of what is good and right and specifically designed for us because we feel we are too late or that circumstances have disqualified us.

Not so.

What you want exists.

What you want is waiting for you.

What you want has always been yours...

You just gotta heal, grow, and keep going until you get it.

Saying things that make others
uncomfortable is uncomfortable.

But betraying yourself by lying about who you are,
what you want, and how you feel can be unbearable.
I have learned that people who truly care about and
value you can handle your truth. This is why it's vital
to only surround yourself with people who care about
and value you. You need a safe space for your truth.

I don't think people talk enough about the
grief that can be associated with outgrowing
things, and especially people. The growth you
desire will require you to change, to let go,
to walk away, and engage in new things.

Your relationships may change.

Your comfortable habits may change.

Your efforts may have to change...

And that's not easy.

But for me, staying the same became harder.

Managing unhealthy relationships, seeing my dreams
go unfulfilled, not walking with purpose and operating
in calling became unbearable. Accepting that no
change meant no growth made it easier to choose
change. If you feel like your growth has been stunted,
it's probably because you haven't embraced change.

You will grow when you embrace the
change that comes with it.

There's so much more to love than
sacrifice, giving, and compromise.

Love is fluid, reciprocal, and a
conduit for wholeness.

Loving others should make you
feel more like yourself, not less.

It should build you up, not tear you down.

It should be a revelation, not a revocation.

Love is where you go to be found, not lost.

Abandon the idea of getting lost in love,
and normalize finding yourself in it.

There are certain people who are assigned
to your life to love you through it all.

Through every version of you, through every season
of growth and change, through moments of chaos and
moments of calm, through the losses and the lessons,
through the success and the glory... You won't come
by a ton of these kinds of people. They show up in
the form of a family member, a life-long friend, or
a love. To have one person like this is a blessing. To
come across more than one may be a miracle. Many
people are struggling because they are chasing after
unrequited love, the love they see others have, the
love they imagined they'd experience by now... When
there is someone, somewhere, already loving them
unconditionally. Stick close to that kind of love.

No more questioning who or what comes and goes.

What left either taught you something or
brought you something for the journey.

What stayed is yours and was uniquely
designed and called in for you.

What's on the way will either be for
you or work for your good.

I have learned to be grateful for it all.

You know you've healed

when you stop seeing your
depression and anxiety as failing

and start seeing it as feeling.

Setting boundaries may make you feel
guilty, mean, and even selfish at first.

Keep setting them.

You'll get used to doing what's best for you.

When you love yourself
You recognize when others ain't loving you right.
You reject fake, conditional, unrequited, and forced love.
You never lack love.
Love finds you.

Holding people accountable to your boundaries
doesn't have to mean you don't love them.

It means you won't love them
more than you love yourself.

Before you can find love
find joy
find peace
find purpose
find success...
You must believe you are worthy of it.

Sometimes strength looks like crying when it hurts, letting go when you've had enough, resting when you're tired, and bending so you don't break. And that is okay.

Notice the ease in making
decisions that aren't influenced
by what other people think.

LIFE IS TOO SHORT TO:

—Focus on things that don't matter.

Preserve your energy for things that move you forward.

—Love people who don't love you.

You deserve the good love you've been giving.
It's okay to expect reciprocity. Find people who
match your love, return your love, and without
question show love, unconditionally.

—Pretend to be happy.

Hiding your true feelings is exhausting.
Stand in your truth so you can create the
happiness you've been longing for.

—Waste time.

You have a purpose. You have a calling. Your time
here on earth should be spent fulfilling those things.

—Settle.

You are worth more than what you've been settling
for. See the value in you and set a standard for
everything and everyone to rise to meet.

During the messiest, most unfortunate, totally confusing, utterly embarrassing, and terribly misunderstood moments in life is when we need that unconditional love that everyone talks about... but rarely shows.

Surround yourself with people who love you right where you are but inspire you to get to where you want to be.

Some people spend a lifetime trying to find themselves. Others spend their lives trying to lose everything that made them think they needed to be found.

You don't need to find yourself. You need to lose the things that make you think who you are, right now, isn't good enough. Lose those fears, the negative self-talk, the comparison, and the concern for what others think... And you'll find yourself— right where you need to be.

SELF-PRESERVATION

You gotta be willing to lose everything and everyone else in your life before you lose yourself. You can always rebuild, there is room to restore, you have the option to replace, and many things can be repaired. But when you lose yourself, you deprive yourself and risk it all. Let there be no guilt in preserving yourself.

People who love and genuinely care for
you will not question your self-care.

They will not be threatened by your growth.

They will not make you feel bad about your boundaries.

They will support your every effort to
heal, grow, and become better.

You will know who's for you because
you will not have to explain that you are
doing what's best for you, to them.

May the same strength you bring to others be returned to you. May the positive words you speak over the lives of others manifest in your life as well. May the wisdom and insight you provide for others give you the clarity you need to navigate your own journey. May your diligence be rewarded, and your work prosper.

Sometimes growth feels like you're losing. Like everything you know, and love is at risk. Like who you were wasn't good enough. Like who you are is a stranger. Growth is good, but the pain that accompanies it can feel bad. Stay committed to your growth. Sometimes your new life will cost you pieces of the old one.

BOUNDARIES

You can love, respect, and have compassion for
someone and still have your boundaries. Boundaries
are for protection, not punishment. They promote
healthy relationships, not pose a threat to them.
Boundaries make what is allowed and expected clear
so the people in your life know how to love you.

It is important to accept the fact that there are some things you just can't control. How and when something will happen will undoubtedly be two of those things. You can decide on what you want. You can even plan and prepare for it, but ultimately that's all you can control. Your job is to make the decision and keep moving forward.

It's tempting to speak your mind when you feel
wronged, or to seek closure when you feel abandoned,
or to explain yourself when you are questioned. But
often you are just exposing your heart to people
you can't trust with it. When your heart is heavy
and you need to express yourself, choose someone
who is worthy of your words and worthy of the
energy it takes to finally say what's on your mind.

STAY CLOSE TO
THINGS THAT:

invite you
excite you
inspire you
revive you
encourage you
challenge you
restore you
heal you
grow you
remind you of who you are

There are parts of your story you had no control over, parts of your story that included people you wish it didn't, parts of your story that has you missing people who are no longer in it, and parts of your story where the part you are playing feels incomplete and unfair. Details aside, the story still belongs to you. It's your story to tell, keep to yourself, and your story to continue co-creating. No matter where you find yourself situated in the middle of your story today, this is just part of your story. Soon you will be able to turn the page.

You are not mean for having boundaries, holding people accountable, and speaking your peace. You are being assertive, responsible, and protective of the life you've built. Don't let up. You get what you accept, and you don't have to accept less than you deserve. Doing what's best for you may be uncomfortable at first. You will adjust, and so will the people who love you.

Someone you can talk to about your feelings, your
past, your goals, your insecurities, your flaws...
and not feel judged should have more of your time.

NAKEIA HOMER is a wellbeing educator, mental wellness advocate, and best-selling author. Her transformative notes, quotes, and indelible messages empower readers around the globe, encouraging them to heal and grow. As a wellbeing expert and trauma-informed educator, Nakeia also facilitates influential workshops and keynotes on the power of story, self-care, and purpose.

nakeiahomer.com